SIGNS
IN OUR WORLD

DK Publishing, Inc.

DK

LONDON, NEW YORK, MUNICH,
MELBOURNE, and DELHI

Writer and Editor : John Searcy
Senior Art Editor : Susan St. Louis
Publishing Director : Beth Sutinis
Art Director : Dirk Kaufman
Production : Ivor Parker
DTP Designer : Kathy Farias

First American Edition, 2006
06 07 08 09 10 10 9 8 7 6 5 4 3 2 1
Published in the United States by DK Publishing, Inc.
375 Hudson Street, New York, New York 10014

DK books are available at special discounts for bulk purchases for sales
promotions, premiums, fund-raising, or educational use. For details, contact:
DK Publishing Special Markets, 375 Hudson Street, New York, New York 10014, SpecialSales@dk.com

Signs in our world.-- 1st American ed., 2006.
    p. cm.
  ISBN 0-7566-1827-4 (pbk.) -- ISBN 0-7566-1834-7 (hardcover)
  1. Traffic signs and signals--Juvenile literature. 2. Street signs--Juvenile literature.
3. Signs and signboards--Juvenile literature.
  TE228.S556 2006
  302.2'22--dc22

2005026849

Color reproduction by Colourscan, Singapore
Printed and bound in China by South China Printing Co., Ltd.

The publisher would like to thank the following for their kind permission to reproduce their images:
a=above; b=bottom/below; c=center; l=left; r=right; t=top

DK Images: Stephen Whitehorn: 7br,
Anthony Limerick: 18cr, David Mager: 23. JupiterImages: 6.
Corbis: 2bl, 9, 11, 13, 18tr, 22c, 27, 30bc, 31a,
corner bolts, Gavriel Jecan: 31b, Steve Terrill: 19b.
Getty Images: 18bl, 18cl, 19a, 21, 29,
Digital Vision: 17, Kevin Jordan: 15, Tim Hall: 24.
Dismar Corporation: 3tr, 25cr/br. Cosco: 25bc.
All other images © Dorling Kindersley
For more information see: www.dkimages.com

Discover more at
www.dk.com

Contents

On the street	4
On the highway	6
Drive carefully	8
Under construction	10
Make way for . . .	12
Danger!	14
Don't do it!	16
Keep it clean	18
In my neighborhood	20
Indoor signs	22
Open for business	24
On the move	26
Outdoor fun	28
By the sea	30

ONE WAY

One-way traffic

This walk signal tells you when to cross the street.

On the street

These signs tell cars and people how to get around on city streets. They help keep everyone moving safely.

Traffic signal ahead

Stop sign

Right turn only

Vehicles do not enter

Right lane ends

Yield sign

Two-way traffic

On the highway

These signs help drivers on the open road. Look out for them next time you're on a long car ride.

NORTH ⑧¹ INTERSTATE 81
Hazleton

Overhead signs tell cars and trucks how to get to different cities.

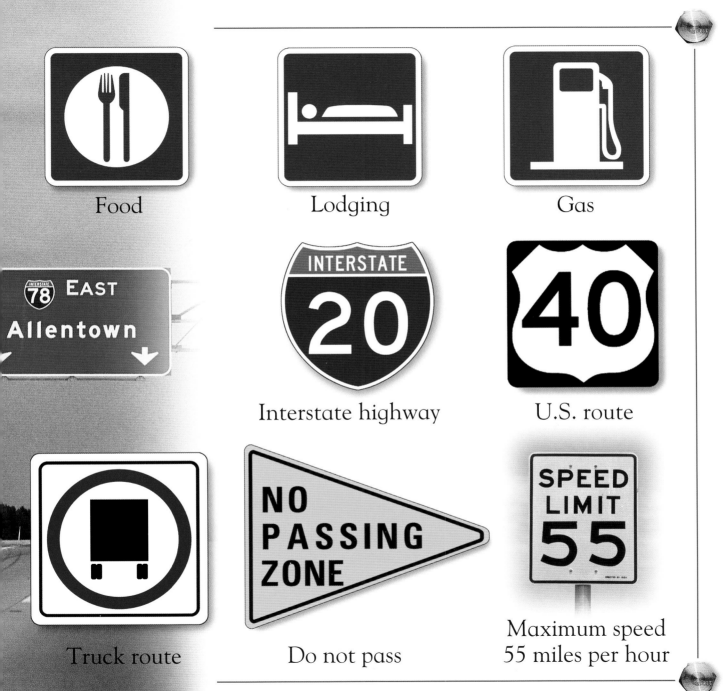

Food

Lodging

Gas

INTERSTATE 78 EAST
Allentown

INTERSTATE 20

Interstate highway

40

U.S. route

Truck route

NO PASSING ZONE

Do not pass

SPEED LIMIT 55

Maximum speed
55 miles per hour

Drive carefully

Driving can be dangerous if you're not careful. These signs help drivers play it safe.

Seat belt reminder

Children playing ahead

Railroad crossing sign

Slippery when wet

Exit: maximum speed 30 miles per hour

Falling rocks

A winding road sign lets you know that the road ahead is going to curve back and forth a lot.

Under construction

If you ever pass through an area where the road is being worked on, you'll probably see some of these signs.

Flagger ahead

Construction monitor ahead

Construction ahead

Surveyors ahead

Workers present

This lane closed

Construction ends here

DETOUR

Detour this way

A road closed sign means the entire street is closed to traffic.

ROAD CLOSED

Make way for . . .

Be careful! These signs warn you about animals and people that might be trying to cross the road ahead of you.

Buffalo crossing

Elk crossing

Burro crossing

Horseback riders

Deer crossing

Ducks crossing

Tractor crossing

Drivers in Australia have to watch out for kangaroos hopping across the road!

Cow crossing

Danger!

These signs either warn you about dangerous conditions or help you take action in an emergency.

Radioactivity

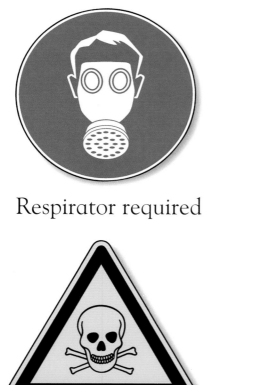
Respirator required

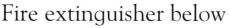
Fire extinguisher below

Slippery floor

Poison

Biohazard symbol

Danger signs can warn you about construction sites where there might be falling debris.

DANGER
HARD HAT AREA

Flammable material

Risk of electric shock

Don't do it!

Hold it right there! Just like parents and teachers, signs are always telling people they're not allowed to do things.

No dogs

No smoking

No left turns

No right turns

No cell phones

No parking

No U-turns

No pedestrians

People put up no trespassing signs when they don't want strangers coming onto their property.

Keep it clean

These signs remind people to keep our world clean and always put garbage in its place.

No throwing trash

Keep beach clean

No dumping in sewer

No littering on highway

Recycling symbol

Waste disposal

Dogs can make
a big mess if
their owners
don't clean up
after them.

In my neighborhood

You might see these signs when you go for a walk. How many can you find near your house?

Police station

Library

Crime watch area

Recommended bike route

School crossing

Crosswalk button

Hospital

This sign invites people to come inside a house to see if they want to buy it.

Playground

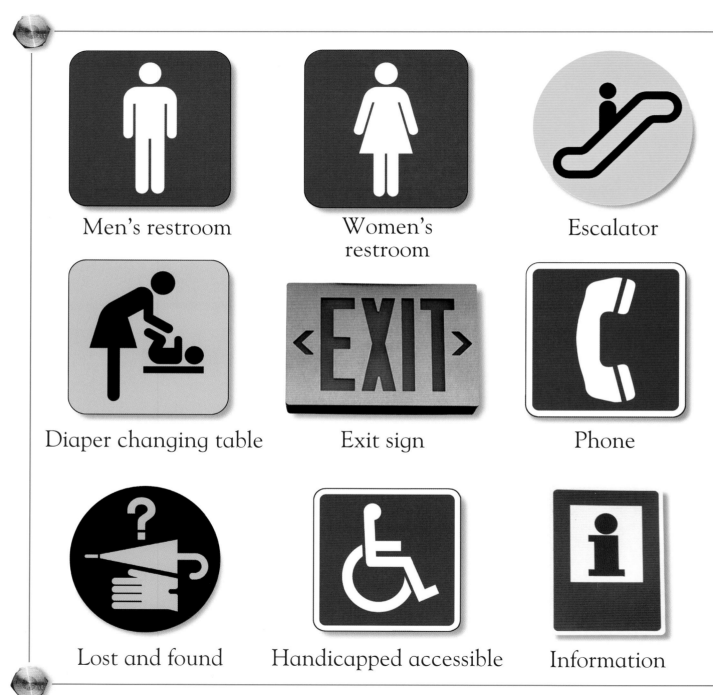

Men's restroom

Women's restroom

Escalator

Diaper changing table

Exit sign

Phone

Lost and found

Handicapped accessible

Information

Indoor signs

These signs are used in malls, airports, and other indoor spaces to help people find the services they need.

This directory sign uses maps to show people where to find different stores at the mall.

Elevator

Open

Come In

An open sign means the store is ready for people to come in and shop!

Open for business

Look for these signs in stores and businesses next time you're out shopping with mom or dad.

Now hiring

Area closed to public

Grand opening banner

Will-return clock

Closed sign

Sale sign

On the move

These are signs you might see when you're on a trip. They help travelers figure out where to go.

Airport

Baggage claim

Passenger pick-up

Ground transportation

Bus stop

Customs

Train station

Ticketing agent

Gate signs help people in airports find the place their plane is leaving from.

Outdoor fun

These signs are common in national parks or anywhere that offers outdoor activities.

Trailer camping

Camping

Boat launch

Ranger station

Fishing

Picnic tables

Campfires permitted

Hiking signs let you know there's a trail nearby where you can take a walk through nature.

Climbing

By the sea

Keep an eye out for these signs next time you're at the beach or on a road near the ocean.

Lighthouse

Strong current

Dangerous shorebreak

Marina

Waterskiing

Surfer crossing

Swimming

This sign warns swimmers that there might be stinging jellyfish in the water!

Find the signs

What sign would you look for if you wanted to . . .

Go camping?

Make a phone call?

Catch a bus?

Borrow a book?

Put out a fire?

Go for a swim?

Pick up your luggage?

Find a lost purse?

Get some lunch?

Catch a fish?

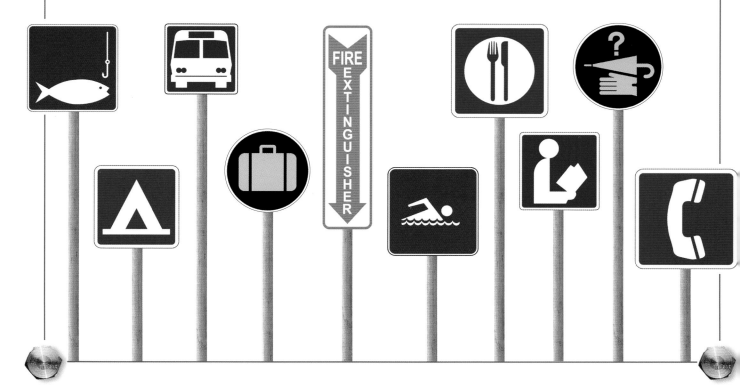